Winter ESSENTIAL KNITS

twelve hand knit designs

quail studio

quail studio

Published in 2015 by
Quail Publishing
The Old Forge,
Market Square,
Toddington
Bedfordshire, LU5 6BP
UK

ISBN: 978-0-9927707-9-2

Conceived, designed and produced by

quail studio

Art Editor: Georgina Brant
Graphic Design: Quail Studio
Technical Editor: Kate Heppell
Photography: Jesse Wild
Creative Director: Darren Brant
Yarn Support: Rowan Yarns
Designer: Quail Studio
Model: Sophie Gibson

Printed in the UK
Second Edition printed March 2017

British Library Cataloguing in Publication Data
A catalogue record for this book is available from the British Library

@quail_studio

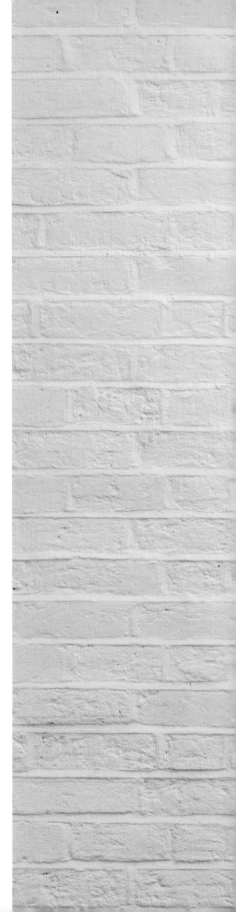

contents

introduction

The first in the series of ESSENTIAL knits from quail studio comes the Winter collection. Designed to be an appealing collection where each design is wearable, and can be styled in different ways – completing your essential winter wardrobe.

The quail studio team have taken simple shapes, paired with a minimalist colour palette and simple styling to bring to life the exquisite yarn from Rowan.

Featuring a core collection of hand knit coats, polo's, sweaters and cardigans accompanied by universal beanie hats, scarf and snood designs.

Hand knit your own essential knitted wardrobe collection, we just know you will not be disappointed!

quail studio team
xoxo

V-NECK
SWEATER
rowan fine lace

CLASSIC POLO
rowan finest

BOYFRIEND
RIB POLO
rowan felted
tweed aran

LONG LINE COAT & SNOOD
rowan brushed fleece

CREW NECK SWEATER
rowan kidsilk haze
& fine lace

CHUNKY
CARDIGAN
rowan brushed fleece

BOYFRIEND CARDIGAN
rowan felted tweed & kidsilk haze

COSY
SCARF
*rowan felted tweed
& kidsilk haze*

MOSS STITCH
BEANIE
rowan felted tweed
& kidsilk haze

STOCKING STITCH BEANIE
rowan brushed fleece

RELAXED
POLO
SWEATER
*rowan super fine
merino aran*

V-NECK Sweater
rowan fine lace

SIZES: XS [S: M: L: XL: XXL]

YARN USAGE: 5 [5: 5: 6: 6: 6] balls of Rowan Fine Lace (shown in SH 922).

NEEDLES: 3mm, 3.25mm (US 3)

TENSION: 26 sts and 32 rows = 10cm measured over st st on larger needles with Rowan Lace held double

PATTERN NOTE: Work with yarn held double throughout.

BACK:
Using 3mm needles and yarn held double, cast on 124 [129: 135: 141: 147: 153] sts.
Work in [K1, P1] rib for 4cm, ending after a WS row.
Change to 3.25mm needles.

Working in st st, decrease 1 st at each end of the 19th row and every foll 20th row until you have
118 [123: 129: 135: 141: 147] sts.
Work 4 rows in st st.
Increase 1 st at each end of 15th row and every following 16th row until you have
124 [129: 135: 141: 147: 153] sts.
Cont straight until work measures
37 [39: 40: 40: 40: 40]cm, ending after a WS row.

SHAPE ARMHOLES:
Cast off 6 sts at beg of next 2 rows.
112 [117: 123: 129: 135: 141] sts.
Dec 1 st at each end of next and
4 following rows. 102 [107: 113: 119: 125: 131] sts.
Dec 1st at each end of next alt row and following 3 alt rows. 94 [99: 105: 111: 117: 123] sts.**

Cont straight until armhole measures 19 [19: 20: 22: 24: 26]cm, ending after a WS row.
Work 28 [30: 33: 36: 39: 42] sts, turn.
Dec 1 st and work to end.
27 [29: 32: 35: 38: 41] sts.
Cast off these 27 [29: 32: 35: 38: 41] sts.
Place centre 38 [39: 39: 39: 39: 39] sts onto a stitch holder or waste yarn.
Rejoin yarn to rem 28 [30: 33: 36: 39: 42] sts and work other side to match.

FRONT:
Work as for back to **.

Cont working straight until front measures 8cm less than back.

SHAPE NECK:
Work 47 [49: 52: 55: 58: 61] sts, turn.
Place rem 47 [50: 53: 56: 59: 62] sts on a stitch holder or waste yarn.
Cont in st st, decrease 1 st at neck edge on next and every following alt row until you have 27 [29: 32: 35: 38: 41] sts.
Cont straight until work measures same as back ending with a WS row.
Cast off.

Rejoin yarn to rem 47 [50: 53: 56: 59: 62] sts, ready to work a RS row.
For sizes XS, M and XL, cast off centre stitch.
For all sizes, work other side to match.

SLEEVES:
Using 3mm needles and yarn held double, cast on 58 [58: 58: 62: 62: 66] sts.
Work in [K1, P1] rib for 4cm, ending after a WS row.

Change to 3.25mm needles.
Working in st st, increase 1 st at each end of 9th and every foll 10th row until you have 84 [84: 84: 88: 88: 92] sts.
Cont straight until work measures 43 [44: 45: 46: 47: 48]cm, ending after a WS row.

SHAPE SLEEVE TOP:
Cast off 6 sts at beg of next 2 rows.
72 [72: 72: 76: 76: 80] sts.
Dec 1 st at each end of next and 4 following rows. 62 [62: 62: 66: 66: 70] sts.
Dec 1 st at each end of next alt row and following 3 alt rows.
54 [54: 54: 58: 58: 62] sts.
Dec 1 st each end of every row until 6 [6: 6: 10: 10: 14] sts remain.
Cast off.

FINISHING:
NECK:
Using 3.25mm needles and yarn held double, with RS facing, pick up and knit 25 sts down left side of neck, 2 sts from gap, 25 sts right side of neck, 2 sts from back neck, knit 38 [39: 39: 39: 39: 39]sts back neck stitch holder, pick up and knit 2 sts across back neck. 94 [95: 95: 95: 95: 95] sts.
Beg with a knit row work 6 rows in st st.
Cast off.

Join other shoulder, set in sleeve and join side and sleeve seams.

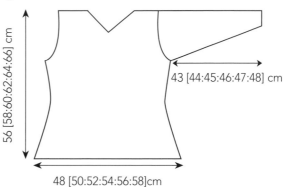

56 [58:60:62:64:66] cm

43 [44:45:46:47:48] cm

48 [50:52:54:56:58]cm

CLASSIC
Polo
rowan finest

SIZES: XS [S: M: L: XL: XXL]

YARN USAGE: 16 [17: 17: 18: 18: 19] balls of Rowan Finest (shown in SH 075).

NEEDLES: 3.25mm (US 3)

TENSION: 28 sts and 36 rows = 10cm measured over st st in Rowan Finest

RIB STITCH:
Row 1: *P3, K1, rep from * to end.
Row 2: *P1, K3, rep from * to end.

BACK:
Using 3.25mm needles, cast on 132 [136: 144: 152: 160: 168] sts
Work in Rib Stitch for 10cm.
Work in st st until work measures 43 [44: 45: 46: 47: 48]cm, ending after a WS row.

SHAPE ARMHOLES:
Cast off 4 sts at beg of next 2 rows.
124 [128: 136: 144: 152: 160] sts.
Dec 1 st at each end of next and following 3 rows. 116 [120: 128: 136: 146: 152] sts.
Dec 1 st at each end of next alt row and following 3 alt rows. 108 [112: 120: 128: 136: 144] sts. **

Cont straight until armhole measures 20 [20: 20: 21: 21: 22]cm, ending after a WS row.
Work 31 [33: 37: 41: 45: 49] sts, turn.
Dec 1 st and work to end.
30 [32: 36: 40: 44: 48] sts.
Cast off.

Place centre 46 sts onto a stitch holder or waste yarn.

Rejoin yarn to rem 31 [33: 37: 41: 45: 49] sts and work other side to match.

FRONT:
Work as for back to **
Continue straight until front measures 8cms less than back.

SHAPE NECK:
Patt 46 [48: 52: 56: 60: 64] sts, turn.
Working in patt, decrease 1 st at neck edge on next 10 rows. 36 [38: 42: 46: 50: 54] sts.
Cont in patt, decreasing at neck edge on every alt row until 30 [32: 36: 40: 44: 48] sts remain.
Cont working straight until front measures same length as back.
Cast off.

Place centre 16 sts onto a stitch holder or waste yarn.
Rejoin yarn to rem 46 [48: 52: 56: 60: 64] sts and work other side of neck to match.

SLEEVES:
Using 3.25mm needles, cast on 56 [64: 64: 72: 72: 80] sts.
Work in Rib Stitch for 8cm.
Work in st st and increase 1 st at each end of 3rd and every following 4th row until you have 112 [120: 120: 128: 128: 136] sts.
Cont straight until work measures 43 [44: 45: 46: 47: 48]cm, ending after a WS row.

SHAPE SLEEVE TOP:
Cast off 4 sts at beg of next 2 rows.
104 [116: 116: 124: 124: 132] sts.
Cont in st st, decrease 1 st at each end of next and following 3 rows.
98 [110: 110: 118: 118: 126] sts.
Dec 1 st at each end of next alt row and following 3 alt rows.

88 [96: 96: 104: 104: 112] sts.
Work one row.
Cast off.

FINISHING:
Join left shoulder seam

NECK:
Using 3.25mm needles and with RS facing, pick up and knit 24 sts down left side of neck, knit 16 across front stitch holder, pick up and knit 24 up right side of neck, 1 st from gap, knit 46 sts across back neck, pick up and knit 1 st from gap. 112 sts.
Work in Rib Stitch for 18cm.
Cast off loosely.

Join other shoulder, set in sleeve and join side and sleeve seams.

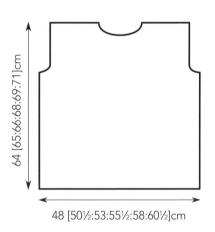

64 [65:66:68:69:71]cm

48 [50½:53:55½:58:60½]cm

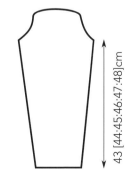

43 [44:45:46:47:48]cm

BOYFRIEND

Rib Polo

*rowan felted
tweed aran*

SIZES: XS [S: M: L: XL: XXL]

YARN USAGE: 13 [14: 14: 15: 16: 17 balls of Felted Tweed Aran (shown in SH 720).

NEEDLES: 5mm (US 8)

TENSION: 15 sts and 24 rows = 10cm measured over patt in felted tweed aran

PATTERN:
Row 1: *K2, P2, rep from * to last 3 sts, K2, P1.

Rep Row 1 for pattern.

BACK:
Using 5mm needles, cast on
87 [91: 95: 99: 103: 107] sts.
Work in pattern until work measures
71 [72: 73: 74: 75: 76]cm, ending after a WS row.

SHAPE BACK NECK:
Patt 27 [29: 31: 33: 35: 37] sts, turn.
Work back across stitches as set.
Cast off.

Place centre 33 sts onto a stitch holder or waste yarn.

Rejoin yarn to rem 27 [29: 31: 33: 35: 37] sts and work other side to match.

FRONT:
Using 5mm needles, cast on
87 [91: 95: 99: 103: 107] sts.
Work in patt until work measures
63 [64: 65: 66: 67: 68: 69]cm, ending after a WS row.

SHAPE NECK:
Patt 38 [40: 42: 44: 46: 48] sts, turn.
Cont working in patt over these sts,

decreasing 1 st at neck edge on next 6 rows. 32 [34: 36: 38: 40: 42] sts.
Cont in patt, decreasing 1 st at neck edge on every alt row until 27 [29: 31: 33:35:37] sts remain.
Cont working in patt until front measures the same length as back.
Cast off.

Place centre 11sts onto a stitch holder or waste yarn.

Rejoin yarn to rem 38 [40: 42: 44: 46: 48] sts and work other side of neck to match.

SLEEVES:
Using 5mm needles, cast on 39 [43: 43: 47: 47 : 51) sts.
Work in patt and increase 1 st at each end of every 6th row until you have 67 [71: 71: 75: 75: 79] sts.
Cont working straight in patt until work measures 41 [42: 43: 44: 45: 46]cm, ending after a WS row.
Cast off.

FINISHING:
Join left shoulder seam.

NECK:
Using 5mm needles and with RS facing, pick up and knit 18 sts down left side of neck, knit 11 sts from front st holder, pick up and knit 18 sts left side of neck, knit 33 sts from back neck holder. 80 sts.

Work in patt for 20cm.

Cast off loosely.

Join other shoulder, set in sleeve and join side and sleeve seams.

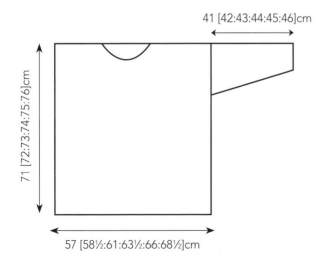

41 [42:43:44:45:46]cm

71 [72:73:74:75:76]cm

57 [58½:61:63½:66:68½]cm

LONG LINE
Coat
rowan brushed fleece

SIZES: XS [S: M: L: XL: XXL]

YARN USAGE: 10 [10: 11: 11: 12: 13] balls of Brushed Fleece (shown in SH 263).

NEEDLES: 6mm (US 10)

TENSION: 15sts and 20 rows = 10cm measured over patt using brushed fleece.

PATTERN:
Row 1: Sl1,*K2, yfwd, sl1, K1, psso, rep from * to last st K1.
Row 2: Sl1,*P2, yrn, P2tog, rep from * to end.

BACK: Using 6mm needles, cast on 90 [94: 98: 102: 106: 110]sts and work 6 rows in garter st.

Work in patt until work measures 94 [96: 98: 100: 102: 104] cm ending after a WS row.

SHAPE BACK NECK:
Patt 33 [35: 37: 39: 41: 43] sts, turn. Work back across stitches as set. Cast off.

Place centre 24 sts onto stitch holder or waste yarn.

Rejoin yarn to rem 33 [35: 37: 39: 41: 43] sts and work other side to match.

LEFT FRONT:
Using 6mm needles, cast on 42 [46: 50: 54: 58: 60] sts. Work 6 rows in garter st.

Work in patt until work measures
84 [86: 88: 90: 92: 94] cm ending after
a RS row.

SHAPE NECK:

Cast off 5 sts, work in patt to end.
37 [41: 45: 49: 53: 55] sts.
Next row: Work in patt to last 2 sts,
work 2 sts tog.
36 [40: 44: 48: 52: 54] sts.
Continue to decrease 1 st at neck
edge on every row until
32 [36: 40: 44: 48: 50] sts rem.
Cont working straight until work
matches length of back.
Cast off.

RIGHT FRONT:

Work as Left Front, reversing
all shapings.

SLEEVES:

Using 6mm needles, cast on
38 [38: 42: 42: 46: 50] sts.
Work 4 rows in garter st.
Work in patt, increasing 1 st at each
end of every 4th row until
70 [70: 74: 74: 78: 81] sts rem.
Cont working straight until work
measures 38 [39: 40: 41: 42: 43] cm,
ending with a WS row.
Cast off.

FINISHING:

Join shoulder seams

FRONT AND NECK BANDS:
LEFT FRONT:

Using a 6mm circular needle and
starting at the top of left front edge
with RS facing, pick up and knit 124
[127: 130: 133: 136: 139] sts along left
front edge.
Work 4 rows in garter st
Cast off loosely.

RIGHT FRONT:

Work as for left front starting at the
base of the right front edge.

NECK:

With RS facing and starting at top of
the right front band:
Pick up and knit 23 sts along right
side of neck, 4 sts from gap, knit 24
sts from back neck, pick up and knit
4 sts from gat, 23 sts down left neck
shaping. 78sts.
Work 4 rows in garter st.
Cast off loosely.
Join side and sleeve seams
Press.

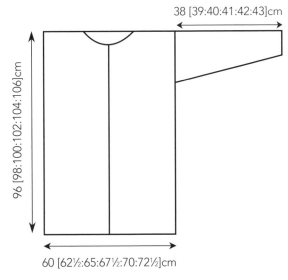

38 [39:40:41:42:43]cm

96 [98:100:102:104:106]cm

60 [62½:65:67½:70:72½]cm

WINTER

Snood

rowan brushed fleece

SIZE: One Size

YARN USAGE: 3 balls of Brushed Fleece (shown in SH 263).

NEEDLES: 6mm (US 10)

TENSION: 15sts and 20 rows = 10cms using Rowan Brushed Fleece

PATTERN:
Row1: Sl1,*K2,yfwd,sl1,k1,psso. Rep from * to last st K1.
Row 2: Sl1,*P2,YRN,P2tog. Rep from * to end.

Using 6mm needles, cast on 42sts and work in pattern until work measures 148cms ending of a WS row.

Cast off.

FINISHING:
Join Cast on and Cast off edges together to make into a snood.

CREW NECK
Sweater

rowan kidsilk haze and fine lace

SIZES: XS [S: M: L: XL: XXL]

YARN USAGE:
3 [3: 3: 3: 3: 4] balls of Rowan Fine Lace (shown in SH 941).

5 [5: 5: 5: 5: 6] balls of Rowan Kidsilk Haze (shown in SH 580).

NEEDLES: 3.25mm (US 3)

TENSION: 26 sts and 32 rows = 10cm measured over st st with one strand each of Rowan Lace and Rowan Kidsilk Haze held together on 3.25mm needles

PATTERN NOTE: Throughout the pattern, hold together one strand each of Rowan Lace and Rowan Kidsilk Haze.

BACK:
Using 3.25mm needles, cast on 118 [124: 130: 136: 142: 148] sts, work in (k2, p2) rib for 4cm.

Work in st st until work measures 40 [42: 44: 45: 46: 47]cm, ending after a WS row.

SHAPE ARMHOLES:
Cont in st st, cast off 4sts at beg of next 2 rows. 110 [116: 122: 128: 136: 140] sts.

Dec 1 st at each end of next and following 4 rows. 100 [106: 112: 118: 126: 130] sts.

Dec 1 st at each end of next alt row and following 2 alt rows. 94 [100: 106: 112: 118: 124] sts. **

Cont straight until armhole measures 20 [20: 20: 21: 22: 23] cm, ending after a WS row.

Work 26 [29: 32: 35: 38] sts, turn.
Dec 1 st and work to end.
25 [28: 31: 34: 37] sts.
Cast off.

Slip centre 42 sts onto a stitch holder
or waste yarn.

Rejoin yarn to rem 26 [29: 32: 35: 38]
sts and work other side to match

FRONT:
Work as for back to **

Cont working straight until front
measures 8cm less than back.

SHAPE NECK:
Patt 40 [43: 46: 49: 52: 55] sts, turn.
Working on these sts only and
keeping patt correct, decrease 1 st at
neck edge on next 8 rows, then cont
to decrease at neck edge on every alt
row until 25 [28: 31: 34: 37: 40] sts rem.
Cont working straight until work is the
same length as back.
Cast off.

Slip centre 14 sts onto a stitch holder
or waste yarn.
Work other side of neck to match.

SLEEVES:
Using 3.25mm needles, cast on
54 [54: 54: 58: 58: 64] sts.
Work in (k2, p2) rib for 4cm.
Work in st st and increase 1 st at each
end of 11th and every foll 12th row
until 78 [78: 78: 84: 84: 88] sts.
Cont straight until work measures
48 [49: 50: 51: 52: 53]cm ending after
a WS row.

SHAPE SLEEVE TOP:
Cast off 4 sts at beg of next 2 rows.
70 [70: 70: 76: 76: 80] sts.
Dec 1 st at each end of next and
following 4 rows.
60 [60: 60: 66: 66: 70] sts.

Dec 1 st at each end of next alt row
and following 2 alt rows.
54 [54: 54: 60: 60: 64] sts.
Dec 1 st at each end of next 22 rows.
10 [10: 10: 16: 16: 20] sts.
Cast off.

FINISHING:
Join left shoulder seam.
NECK:
Using 3.25mm needles and RS facing,
pick up and knit 29 sts down left side
of neck, knit 14 sts across front st
holder, picuk up and knit 29 sts right
side of neck, 2 sts from back neck, knit
42 sts back neck stitch holder, pick up
and knit 2 sts across back neck.118 sts.
Beg with a knit row, work 6 rows in
st st.
Cast off.

Join other shoulder, set in sleeve and
join side and sleeve seams.

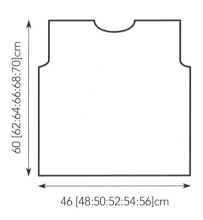

60 [62:64:66:68:70]cm

46 [48:50:52:54:56]cm

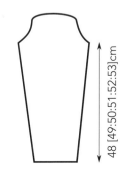

48 [49:50:51:52:53]cm

CHUNKY
Cardigan
rowan brushed fleece

SIZES: XS [S: M: L: XL: XXL]

YARN USAGE: 9 [9: 10: 10: 11: 12] balls of Brushed Fleece (shown in SH 253).

BUTTONS: 6 medium sized buttons.

NEEDLES: 5mm (US 8), 6mm (US 10)

TENSION: 13sts and 19rows = 10cm measured over st st in Brushed Fleece using larger needles.

BACK:
Using 5mm needles, cast on
70 [73: 76: 79: 82: 85] sts.
Work in moss st for 6cm.
Change to 6mm needles.
Work in st st until work measures
46 [48: 50: 51: 53: 54]cm, ending after a WS row.

SHAPE ARMHOLES:
Cast off 3sts at beg of next 2 rows.
64 [67: 70: 73: 76: 79] sts.
Dec 1 st at each end of every alt row 3 times. 58 [61: 64: 67: 70: 73] sts.
Cont working straight in st st until armhole measures 22 [22: 22: 23: 23: 24]cm, ending after a WS row.

SHAPE SHOULDERS:
Work 16 [17: 19: 20: 21: 22] sts in patt, turn.
Work back across stitches as set.
Cast off these 16 [17: 19: 20: 21: 22] sts.
Place centre 26 [27: 26: 27: 28: 29] sts onto stitch holder or waste yarn.
Rejoin yarn to rem 16 [17: 19: 20: 21: 22] sts for opposite shoulder and work to match first side.

LEFT FRONT:
Using 5mm needles, cast on
32 [34: 36: 38: 40: 42] sts.
Work in moss st for 6cm.
Change to 6mm needles.
Work in st st until work measures
46 [48: 50: 51: 53: 54]cm, ending after
a WS row.

SHAPE ARMHOLE:
Cast off 3 sts at beg of next row, work
to end. 29 [31: 33: 35: 37: 39] sts.
Dec 1st at the beg of every foll alt row
3 times. 26 [28: 30: 32: 34: 36] sts.
Cont working straight until work
measures 57 [59: 61: 63: 65: 67]cm,
ending after a RS row.

SHAPE NECK:
Cast off 5sts, work in patt to end.
Next row: Work in patt to last 2
stitches, Work 2 sts tog.
20 [22: 24: 26: 28: 30] sts.
Continue to decrease one st at neck
edge on every row until
13 [15: 17: 19: 21: 23] sts rem.
When work matches length of back
Cast off.

RIGHT FRONT:
Work as Left Front, reversing
all shapings.

SLEEVES:
Using 5mm needles, cast on
32 [32: 34: 36: 38: 40] sts.
Work 6cm in moss st.
Change to 6mm needles.
Work in st st, increasing 1 st at each
end of 7th and every foll 6th row until
58 [58: 60: 62: 64: 66] sts.
Cont straight until work measures
44 [45: 46: 47: 48: 49] cm, ending after
a WS row.

SHAPE SLEEVE TOP:
Cast off 3sts at beg of next 2 rows.
52 [52: 54: 56: 58: 60] sts.

Dec 1 st at each end of every foll alt
row 3 times. 46 [46: 48: 50: 52: 54] sts.
Work one row,
Cast off.

FINISHING:
Join shoulder seams

FRONT AND NECK BANDS:
LEFT FRONT: (BUTTONHOLE BAND)
Using a 5mm circular needle starting
at the top of left front edge and
RS facing,

Pick up and knit 78(80:82:86:86:88)sts
along left front edge.

Work 5 rows in moss st,

Next row (buttonhole row): work
3(4:5:2:2:3) sts *Yfwd, sl1,k1,psso, work
12(:12:12:14:14:14) sts, rep from * to
last 5(6:7:4:4:5)sts, Yfwd, sl1, k1, psso,
work to end.

Work a further 3 rows in moss st,

Cast off.

RIGHT FRONT: (BUTTONBAND)
Using a 5mm circular needle starting
at the base of the right front edge
and RS facing,

Pick up and knit 78(80:82:86:86:88)sts
along left front edge.

Work 9 rows in moss st.

Cast off.

COLLAR:

With RS facing and starting at top of the right front band: Pick up and knit 30sts along right side of neck, 2 sts from gap, knit 26 [27: 26: 27: 28: 29] sts across back stitch holder, pick up and knit 2 sts from gap, 30 sts down left neck shaping.
90 [91: 90: 91: 92: 93] sts.
Work 14cms in moss st.
Cast off.

Set in sleeves, Join side and sleeve seams.
Press.
Sew on the buttons.

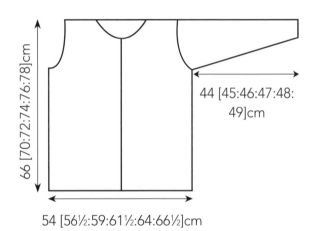

66 [70:72:74:76:78]cm

44 [45:46:47:48: 49]cm

54 [56½:59:61½:64:66½]cm

BOYFRIEND
Cardigan
rowan felted tweed and kidsilk haze

SIZES: XS [S: M: L: XL: XXL]

YARN USAGE:
8 [8: 9: 9: 10: 11] balls of Rowan Felted Tweed (shown in SH 157).

6 [6: 7: 7: 8: 9] balls of Rowan Kidsilk Haze (shown in SH 672).

NEEDLES: 4mm straight (US 6), 4mm circular (80cm) (US 6)

TENSION: 21 sts and 28 rows = 10cm measured over st st with one strand each of Rowan Felted Tweed and Rowan Kidsilk Haze held together.

PATTERN NOTE: Use one strand each of Rowan Felted Tweed and Rowan Kidsilk Haze held together throughout the pattern.

RIB PATTERN:
Row 1: * K1, P3, rep from * to last 2 sts, K1, P1.
Row 2: K1, p1,*K3, P1, rep from * to end.

BACK:
Using 4mm needles and with one strand each of Rowan Felted Tweed and Rowan Kidsilk Haze held together, cast on 126 [130: 134: 142: 146: 150] sts.

Work in rib pattern for 8cm, ending after a WS row.

Work in st st until work measures 54 [55: 56: 53: 54: 53]cm, ending after a WS row.

SHAPE RAGLAN:
Cast off 6 [6: 8: 8: 10: 10] sts at the beg of next 2 rows. 114 [118: 118: 126: 126: 130] sts.

Dec 1 st at each end of next and every following alt row until 42 [46: 46: 46: 46: 46] sts remain.

At this point, the back should measure approx 79 [80: 81: 82: 83: 84]cm.

Cast off.

LEFT FRONT:
Using 4mm needles and with one strand each of Rowan Felted Tweed and Rowan Kidsilk Haze held together, cast on 62 [66: 70: 74: 78: 82] sts.

Work in rib pattern for 8cm, ending after a WS row.

Work in st st until work measures 14 [14: 14: 18: 18: 22] rows before raglan shaping of back, ending after a RS row.

SHAPE NECK:
Dec 1 st at neck edge on next and every following 4th row. **AT THE SAME TIME:** When work measures 54 [55: 56: 53: 54: 53]cm, ending after a WS row, begin working raglan shaping as follows;

SHAPE RAGLAN:
Cast off 6 [6: 8: 8: 10: 10] sts at beg of next row.
Purl one row.
Dec 1 st at beg of next and following alt rows.
Continue with both raglan and neck shaping until 1 st remains. Fasten off.

RIGHT FRONT:
Work as Left Front, reversing all shapings.

SLEEVES:
Using 4mm needles and with one strand each of Rowan Felted Tweed and Rowan Kidsilk Haze held together, cast on 42 [42: 46: 46: 50: 54] sts.

Work in rib pattern for 8cm, ending after a WS row.

Working in st st, increase 1 st at each end of 3rd and every following 4th (4th: 4th: 3rd: 3rd: 3rd] row until you have 92 [92: 92: 106: 110: 114] sts.

Cont straight until work measures 43 [44: 45: 43: 44: 43]cm, ending after a WS row.

SHAPE RAGLAN:
Cast off 6 [6: 8: 8: 10: 10] sts at beg of next 2 rows. 80 [80: 76: 90: 90: 94] sts.
Dec 1st each end of next and every alternate row until 10 sts remain.
Cast off.

FINISHING:
Join all raglans

FRONT AND NECK BANDS:
LEFT FRONT AND NECK:
Using a 4mm circular needle and with one strand each of Rowan Felted Tweed and Rowan Kidsilk Haze held together, starting at the centre of the back neck with RS facing, pick up and knit 19 sts along back neck, 10 sts across top of sleeve, 58 sts down left front neck shaping, 82 [84: 86: 88: 90: 92] sts along left front edge.
169 [171: 173: 175: 177: 179] sts.
Work 5 rows in [K2, P2] rib.
Starting with a knit row, work 4 rows in st st.
Cast off loosely.

RIGHT FRONT AND NECK:

With RS facing and starting at lower edge of right front:

Pick up and knit 82 [84: 86: 88: 90: 92] sts along right front edge, 58 sts down right front neck shaping, 10 sts across top of sleeve, 19 sts along back neck.
169 [171: 173: 175: 177: 179] sts.
Work 5 rows in [K2, P2] rib.
Starting with a knit row, work 4 rows in st st.
Cast off loosely.

Join at back neck, join side and sleeve seams.

Press.

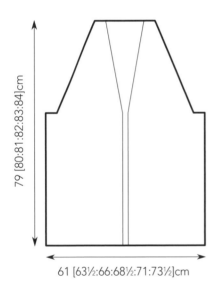

79 [80:81:82:83:84]cm

61 [63½:66:68½:71:73½]cm

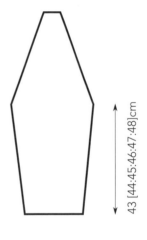

43 [44:45:46:47:48]cm

COSY

Scarf

rowan kidsilk haze and felted tweed

SIZE: One Size (approx 28cm x 212cm).

YARN USAGE:
4 balls of Rowan Kidsilk Haze (shown in SH 642).
5 balls of Rowan Felted Tweed (shown in SH 191).

NEEDLES: 9mm (US 13)

TENSION:
Working 2 ends of Felted tweed and 2 ends
of Kidsilk haze together on a 9mm needle and
working in Moss St: 15sts and 20 rows = 10cms.

PATTERN:
Using 9mm needles, cast on 37sts and work in
single moss st until work measures 212cms.
Cast off.

MOSS STITCH
Beanie

rowan kidsilk haze and felted tweed

SIZE: One Size

YARN USAGE:
1 ball of Rowan Kidsilk Haze (shown in SH 642).
2 balls of Rowan Felted Tweed (shown in SH 191).

NEEDLES: 9mm (US 13)

TENSION: 15sts and 20rows = 10cm measured over moss st using 2 ends of Felted tweed and 2 ends of Kidsilk haze together

PATTERN:
Using 9mm needles cast on 51sts work 6 rows in K1 P1 rib.

Work in single moss st until work measures 18 cm ending after a WS row.

SHAPE TOP:
Patt 4, sl1, k2tog, psso, *patt 7, sl1, k2tog, psso rep from * to end. (41sts)
Next row: patt across all sts.
Patt 3, sl1, k2tog, psso *patt 5, sl1, k2tog, psso rep from * to end. (31sts)
Next row: part across all sts.
Patt 2, sl1, k2tog, psso, *patt 3, sl1, k2tog, psso rep from * to end. (21sts)
Next row: patt across all sts.
Patt 1, sl1, k2tog, psso *patt 1, sl1, k2tog, psso rep from * to end. (11sts)

FINISHING:
Cut yarn and thread back through sts on the needle. Pull and secure by stitching.

Join side seam.

Add a Pom Pom of your choice.

STOCKING STITCH *Beanie*

rowan brushed fleece

SIZE: One Size

YARN USAGE:
1 ball of Brushed Fleece
(shown in SH 263).

NEEDLES: 6mm (US 10)

TENSION: 13sts and 19rows = 10cm
measured over stst using brushed fleece.

PATTERN:
Using 6mm needles, cast on 55sts and
work 6 rows in K1 P1 rib.
Work in st st until work measures 18 cm
ending after a WS row.

SHAPE TOP:
K4*sl1,k2tog, psso, k8. Rep from * to last
4sts, k4. (45sts)
Next row; purl

K3*sl1,k2tog, psso, k6. Rep from * to last
3sts, k3. (35sts)
Next row; purl
K2*sl1,k2tog, psso, k4. Rep from * to last
2sts, k2. (25sts)
Next row; purl
K1*sl1,k2tog, psso. Rep from * to end
(9sts)

FINISHING:
Cut yarn and thread back through sts on
the needle. Pull and secure by stitching.

Join side seam.

Add a Pom Pom of your choice.

RELAXED POLO
Sweater

rowan super fine merino aran

SIZES: XS [S: M: L: XL: XXL]

YARN USAGE: 17 [18: 18: 19: 20: 21] balls of Rowan Superfine Aran (shown in SH 002).

NEEDLES: 4.5mm (US 7), 5mm (US 8)

TENSION: 19 sts and 25 rows = 10cm measured over st st in Superfine Aran using larger needles.

RIB STITCH:
Row 1: K2, *P3, K2, rep from * to end
Row 2: P2, *K1, P1, K1, P2, rep from * to end.

BACK:
Using 4.5mm needles, cast on 102 [107: 112: 117: 122: 127] sts.

Work in Rib Stitch for 13cm, ending after a WS row.

Change to 5mm needles.

Work in st st until work measures 46 [47: 48: 49: 50: 51]cm, ending after a WS row.

SHAPE ARMHOLES:
Cast off 3 sts at beg of next 2 rows. 96 [101: 106: 111: 116: 121] sts.

Dec 1 st at each end of next and following row. 92 [97: 102: 107: 112: 117] sts.

Dec 1st at each end of next and following alt row. 88 [93: 98: 103: 108: 113] sts.

Cont working straight until armhole measures 23 [23: 23: 24: 24: 24]cm, ending after a WS row.
Work 26 [28: 31: 33: 36: 38] sts, turn.
Dec 1 st and work to end.
25 [27: 30: 32: 35: 37] sts.
Cast off.

Place centre 36 [37: 36: 37: 36: 37) sts onto a stitch holder or waste yarn.
Rejoin yarn to rem 26 [28: 31: 33: 36: 38] sts and work other side to match.

FRONT:
Using 4.5mm needles, cast on 102 [107: 112: 117: 122: 127] sts.
Work in Rib Stitch for 10cm, ending after a WS row.
Change to 5mm needles and work in st st until work measures 43 [44: 45: 46: 47: 48]cm, ending after a WS row.

SHAPE ARMHOLES:
Cast off 3 sts at beg of next 2 rows.
96 [101: 106: 111: 116: 121] sts.

Dec 1 st at each end of next and following row. 92 [97: 102: 107: 112: 117] sts.

Dec 1st at each end of next and following alt row. 88 [93: 98: 103: 108: 113] sts.

Continue straight until armhole measures 15 [15: 15: 16: 16: 16]cm.

SHAPE NECK:
Patt 38 [40, 43, 45, 48, 50] sts, turn.
Working on these sts only, decrease 1 st at neck edge on next 8 rows.
30 [32: 35: 37: 40: 42] sts.
Decrease 1 st at neck edge on every alt row until 25 [27: 30: 32: 35: 37] sts remain.
Cont working straight until armhole measures same length as back armhole, ending after a WS row.
Cast off.

Place centre 12 [13: 12: 13: 12: 13] sts onto a stitch holder or waste yarn.

Rejoin yarn to rem 38 [40: 43: 45: 48: 50] sts and work other side of neck to match.

SLEEVES:
Using 4.5mm needles, cast on 47 [47: 47: 52: 52: 57] sts.
Work in Rib Stitch for 10cm, ending after a WS row.

Change to 5mm needles.

Work in st st, inc 1 st at each end of 3rd and every following 4th row until you have 87 [87: 87: 92: 92: 97] sts.
Cont straight until work measures 43 [44: 45: 46: 47: 48]cm, ending after a WS row.

SHAPE SLEEVE TOP:
Cast off 3sts at beg of next 2 rows.
81 [81: 81: 86: 96: 91] sts.
Dec 1 st at each end of next and following row.
77 [77: 77: 82: 82: 87] sts.
Dec 1 st at each end of next and following alt row. 73 [73: 73: 78: 78: 83] sts.
Work one row.
Cast off.

FINISHING:
NECK:
Using 4.5mm needles and with RS facing, pick up and knit 18 sts down left side of neck, knit 12 [13: 12: 13: 12: 13] sts across front st holder, pick up and knit 19 sts along right side of neck, 1 st from gap, knit 36 [37: 36: 37: 36: 37] sts back neck stitch holder, pick up and knit 1 st from gap. 87 [89: 87: 89: 87: 89] sts.
Work in rib pattern for 20 cm.
Cast off in rib.

Join other shoulder, set in sleeve and join side and sleeve seams.

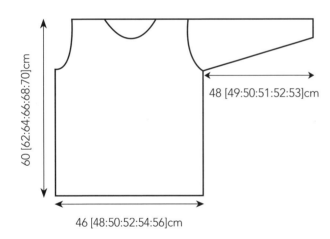

60 [62:64:66:68:70]cm

48 [49:50:51:52:53]cm

46 [48:50:52:54:56]cm

Abbreviations

K – knit
P – purl
st(s) – stitch(es)
inc – increas(e)(ing)
dec – decreas(e)(ing)
st st – stocking stitch (1 row knit, 1 row purl)
g st – garter stitch (every row knit)
beg – begin(ning)
foll – following
rem – remain(ing)
alt – alternate
cont – continue
patt – pattern
tog – together
mm – millimetres
cm – centimetres
in – inch(es)
RS – right side
WS – wrong side
sl 1 – slip one stitch
psso – pass slipped stitch over
tbl – through back of loop
m1 – make one stitch by picking up loop between last and next stitch and working into the back of this loop
yfwd - bring yarn forward between the needles and then back over before making the next stitch.
yrn – yarn round needle. Wrap yarn around the needle back to a purl posistion.

ROWAN STOCKISTS

AUSTRALIA: Australian Country Spinners, Pty Ltd, Level 7, 409 St. Kilda Road,Melbourne Vic 3004. Tel: 03 9380 3888 Fax: 03 9820 0989 Email: customerservice@auspinners.com.au

AUSTRIA: Coats Harlander Ges.m.b.H.., Autokaderstraße 29, 1210 Wien, Austria Tel: 00800 26 27 28 00 Fax: (00) 49 7644 802-133 Email: coats.harlander@coats.com Web: www.coatscrafts.at

BELGIUM: Coats N.V., c/o Coats GmbH Kaiserstr.1 79341 Kenzingen Germany Tel: 0032 (0) 800 77 89 2 Fax: 00 49 7644 802 133 Email: sales.coatsninove@coats.com Web: www.coatscrafts.be

BULGARIA: Coats Bulgaria, 7 Magnaurska Shkola Str., BG-1784 Sofia, Bulgaria Tel: (+359 2) 976 77 41 Fax: (+359 2) 976 77 20 Email: officebg@coats.com Web: www.coatsbulgaria.bg

CANADA: Westminster Fibers, 10 Roybridge Gate, Suite 200, Vaughan, Ontario L4H 3M8 Tel: (800) 263-2354 Fax: 905-856-6184 Email: info@westminsterfibers.com

CHINA: Coats Shanghai Ltd, No 9 Building , Baosheng Road, Songjiang Industrial Zone, Shanghai. Tel: (86- 21) 13816681825 Fax: (86-21) 57743733-326 Email: victor.li@coats.com

CYPRUS: Coats Bulgaria, 7 Magnaurska Shkola Str., BG-1784 Sofia, Bulgaria Tel: (+359 2) 976 77 41 Fax: (+359 2) 976 77 20 Email: officebg@coats.com Web: www.coatscrafts.com.cy

CZECH REPUBLIC: Coats Czecho s.r.o.Staré Mesto 246 569 32Tel: (420) 461616633 Email: galanterie@coats.com

ESTONIA: Coats Eesti AS, Ampri tee 9/4, 74001 Viimsi HarjumaaTel: +372 630 6250 Fax: +372 630 6260 Email: info@coats.ee Web: www.coatscrafts.co.ee

DENMARK: Carl J. Permin A/S Egegaardsvej 28 DK-2610 Rødovre Tel: (45) 36 72 12 00 E-mail: permin@permin.dk

FINLAND: Coats Opti Crafts Oy, Huhtimontie 6 04200 KERAVA Tel: (358) 9 274871 Email: coatsopti.sales@coats.com www.coatscrafts.fi

FRANCE: Coats France, c/o Coats GmbH, Kaiserstr.1, 79341 Kenzingen, Germany Tel: (0) 0810 06 00 02 Email: artsdufil@coats.com Web: www.coatscrafts.fr

GERMANY: Coats GmbH, Kaiserstr. 1, 79341 Kenzingen, Germany Tel: 0049 7644 802 222 Email: kenzingen.vertrieb@coats.com Fax: 0049 7644 802 30 Web: www.coatsgmbh.de

GREECE: Coats Bulgaria, 7 Magnaurska Shkola Str., BG-1784 Sofia, Bulgaria Tel: (+359 2) 976 77 41 Fax: (+359 2) 976 77 20 Email: officebg@coats.com Web: www.coatscrafts.gr

HOLLAND: Coats B.V., c/o Coats GmbH, Kaiserstr.1, 79341 Kenzingen, Germany Tel: 0031 (0) 800 02 26 6488 Fax: 00 49 7644 802 133 Email: sales.coatsninove@coats.com Web: www.coatscrafts.be

HONG KONG: East Unity Company Ltd, Unit B2, 7/F., Block B, Kailey Industrial Centre, 12 Fung Yip Street, Chai Wan Tel: (852)2869 7110 Email: eastunityco@yahoo.com.hk

ICELAND: Storkurinn, Laugavegi 59, 101 Reykjavik Tel: (354) 551 8258 Email: storkurinn@simnet.is

ITALY: Coats Cucirini srl, Viale Sarca no 223, 20126 Milano Tel: 02636151 Fax: 0266111701

KOREA: Coats Korea Co. Ltd, 5F Eyeon B/D, 935-40 Bangbae-Dong, 137-060 Tel: (82) 2 521 6262 Fax: (82) 2 521 5181 Email: rozenpark@coats.com

LATVIA: Coats Latvija SIA, Mukusalas str. 41 b, Riga LV-1004 Tel: +371 67 625173 Fax: +371 67 892758 Email: info.latvia@coats.com Web: www.coatscrafts.lv

LEBANON: y.knot, Saifi Village, Mkhalissiya Street 162, BeirutTel: (961) 1 992211 Fax: (961) 1 315553 Email: y.knot@cyberia.net.lb

LITHUANIA & RUSSIA: Coats Lietuva UAB, A. Juozapaviciaus str. 6/2, LT-09310 Vilnius Tel: +370 527 30971 Fax: +370 527 2305 Email: info@coats.lt Web: www.coatscrafts.lt

LUXEMBOURG: Coats N.V., c/o Coats GmbH, Kaiserstr.1, 79341 Kenzingen, Germany Tel: 00 49 7644 802 222 Fax: 00 49 7644 802 133 Email: sales.coatsninove@coats.com Web: www.coatscrafts.be

MALTA: John Gregory Ltd, 8 Ta'Xbiex Sea Front, Msida MSD 1512, Malta Tel: +356 2133 0202 Fax: +356 2134 4745 Email: raygreg@onvol.net

MEXICO: Estambres Crochet SA de CV, Aaron Saenz 1891-7, PO Box SANTAMARIA, 64650 MONTERREY TEL +52 (81) 8335-3870

NEW ZEALAND: ACS New Zealand, P.O. Box 76199, Northwood, Christchurch New Zealand Tel: 64 3 323 6665 Fax: 64 3 323 6660 Email: lynn@impactmg.co.nz

NORWAY: Falk Knappehuset AS, Svinesundsveien 347, 1788 Halden, Norway Tel: +47 555 393 00 Email: post@falkgruppen.no

PORTUGAL: Coats & Clark, Quinta de Cravel, Apartado 444, 4431-968 Portugal Tel: 00 351 223 770700

SINGAPORE: Golden Dragon Store, 101 Upper Cross Street #02-51, People's Park Centre, Singapore 058357 Tel: (65) 6 5358454 Fax: (65) 6 2216278 Email: gdscraft@hotmail.com

SLOVAKIA: Coats s.r.o.Kopcianska 94851 01 Bratislava Tel: (421) 263532314 Email: galanteria@coats.com

SOUTH AFRICA: Arthur Bales LTD, 62 4th Avenue, Linden 2195 Tel: (27) 11 888 2401 Fax: (27) 11 782 6137 Email: arthurb@new.co.za

SPAIN: Coats Fabra SAU, Avda Meridiana 350, pta 13, 08027 Barcelona Tel: (34) 932908400 Fax: 932908409 Email: atencion.clientes@coats.com

SWEDEN: Bröderna Falk Sybehör & Garn Engros, Stationsvägen 2, 516 31 Dalsjöfors Tel: (46) 40-6084002 Fax: 033-7207940 Email: kundtjanst@falk.se

SWITZERLAND: Coats Stroppel AG, Stroppelstrasse 20, 5417 Untersiggenthal, Switzerland Tel: 00800 2627 2800 Fax: 0049 7644 802 133 Email: coats.stroppel@coats.com Web: www.coatscrafts.ch

TAIWAN: Cactus Quality Co Ltd, 7FL-2, No. 140, Sec.2 Roosevelt Rd, Taipei, 10084 Taiwan, R.O.C. Tel: 00886-2-23656527 Fax: 886-2-23656503 Email: cqcl@ms17.hinet.net

THAILAND: Global Wide Trading, 10 Lad Prao Soi 88, Bangkok 10310 Tel: 00 662 933 9019 Fax: 00 662 933 9110 Email: global.wide@yahoo.com

U.S.A.: Westminster Fibers, 8 Shelter Drive, Greer, South Carolina, 29650 Tel: (800) 445-9276 Fax: 864-879-9432 Email: info@westminsterfibers.com

U.K: Rowan, Green Lane Mill, Holmfirth, West Yorkshire, England HD9 2DX Tel: +44 (0) 1484 681881 Fax: +44 (0) 1484 687920 Email: ccuk.sales@coats.com Web: www.knitrowan.com

Information

TENSION

This is the size of your knitting. Most of the knitting patterns will have a tension quoted. This is how many stitches 10cm/4in in width and how many rows 10cm/4in in length to make a square. If your knitting doesn't match this then your finished garment will not measure the correct size. To obtain the correct measurements for your garment you must achieve the tension.

The tension quoted on a ball band is the manufacturer's average. For the manufacturer and designers to produce designs they have to use a tension for you to be able to obtain the measurements quoted. It's fine not to be the average, but you need to know if you meet the average or not. Then you can make the necessary adjustments to obtain the correct measurements.

YARN

Keep one ball band from each project so that you have a record of what you have used and most importantly how to care for your garment after it has been completed. Always remember to give the ball band with the garment if it is a gift.

The ball band normally provides you with the average tension and recommended needle sizes for the yarn, this may vary from what has been used in the pattern, always go with the pattern as the designer may change needles to obtain a certain look. The ball band also tells you the name of the yarn and what it is made of, the weight and approximate length of the ball of yarn along with the shade and dye lot numbers. This is important as dye lots can vary, you need to buy your yarn with matching dye lots.

PRESSING AND AFTERCARE

Having spent so long knitting your project it can be a great shame not to look after it properly. Some yarns are suitable for pressing once you have finished to improve the look of the fabric. To find out this information you will need to look on the yarn ball band, where there will be washing and care symbols.

Once you have checked to see if your yarn is suitable to be pressed and the knitting is a smooth texture (stocking stitch for example), pin out and place a damp cloth onto the knitted pieces. Hold the steam iron (at the correct temperature) approximately 10cm/4in away from the fabric and steam. Keep the knitted pieces pinned in place until cool.

As a test it is a good idea to wash your tension square in the way you would expect to wash your garment.

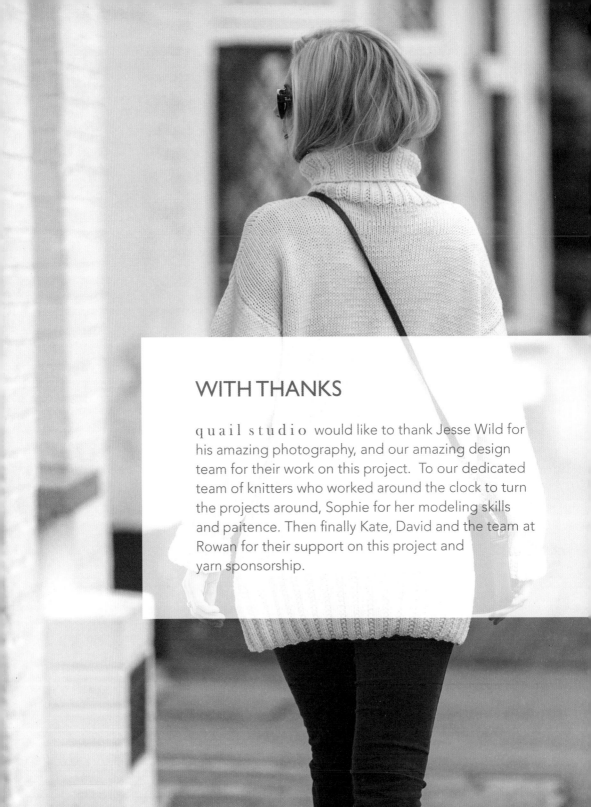

WITH THANKS

q u a i l s t u d i o would like to thank Jesse Wild for
his amazing photography, and our amazing design
team for their work on this project. To our dedicated
team of knitters who worked around the clock to turn
the projects around, Sophie for her modeling skills
and paitence. Then finally Kate, David and the team at
Rowan for their support on this project and
yarn sponsorship.